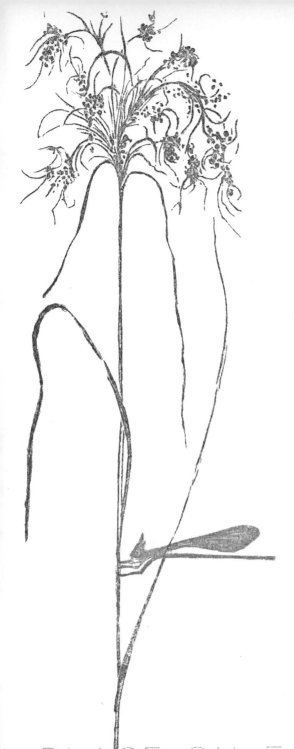

A PLACE ON EARTH

Gwen Frostic

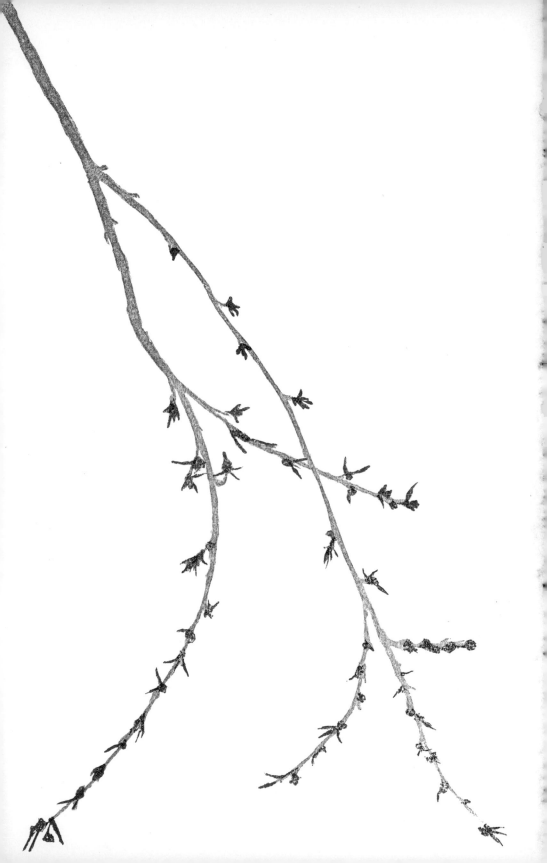

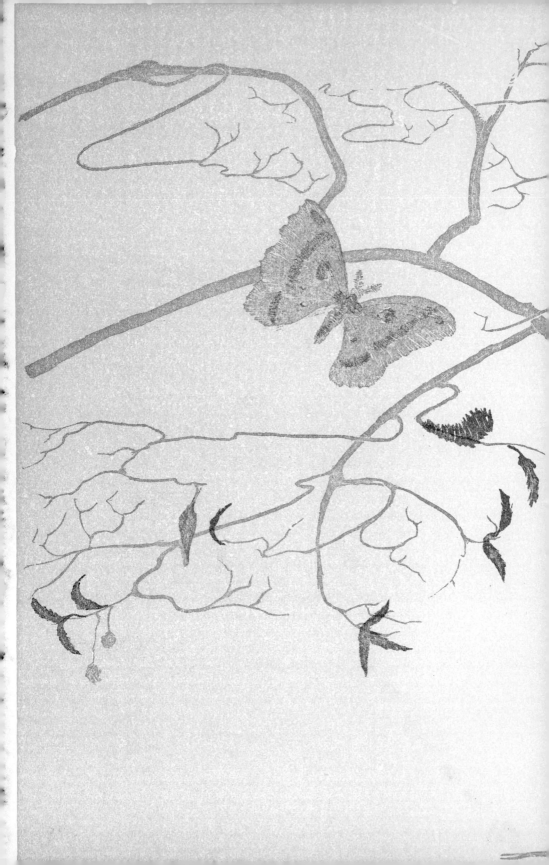

Each frog - - -   and insect
                bird - - -   and tree
and everything that lives and breathes
        somehow creates its place on earth . . .

The plants need water to survive
                in turn give water to the sky - -
a blue jay feeds upon the nuts
                of trees that jays have planted - - -

the moth that pollinates the flowers
        once ate the leaves - -   before it flew

As each thing ever fosters
                the thing that fosters it

- - - - and in return must ever give
        as much as it receives - - - - -

that all things shall keep a perfect balance
        and earn a place on earth . . . .

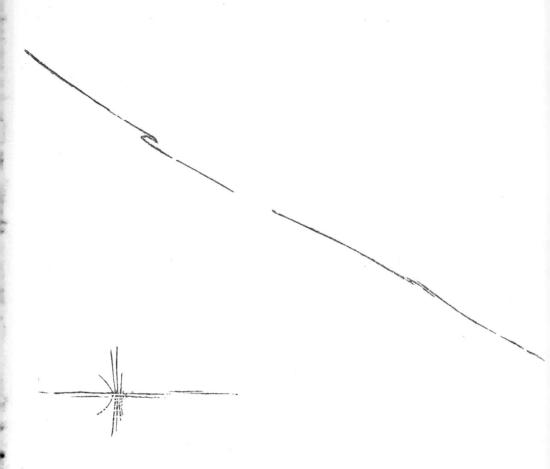

Over the swamp comes a long low call
    the wind in the trees and the birds are free - - ·
Part of my soul answers to that call - - - - - -
    in my heart beats the rhythm
               of the wind and the wings
  and I am at one with loveliness . . . .

From the time the first skunk cabbage
pushes its way through the snows of spring - - -
- - - until snow comes again and covers the last
dandelion of fall - - - - - -

the glory of flowers is everywhere

wondrous in its loveliness

and its diversity . . . . . .

In rivers and pools - - - - swamplands and
woodland glens - - - across the dunes and in
the sunlit meadows - - - - life - - with all its
beauty - - - its achievement over adversity - - its
promise of eternity - - - is taking place . . . . .

Here are living cells continuously dividing with
streaming movements along fine threads within the
plants - - - cells whose chemical reaction is so
directed that each plant shall grow and reproduce
its own . . . .

A little green shoot that has risen from the earth - - - now free to ascend - - - within the realm of its kind - - - - to whatever beauty it may attain . . . .

It breathes - - - as all living things must do - - it drinks - - - it must rest - - - and above all it must grow - - - - - for if it ceases to grow - - it shall cease to live . . . .

Everything about the little plant has meaning - - - - the shape of its leaves - - - their position on its stem - - the color and fragrance of its blossoms - - - - - - - all things are constantly and consistently working together to produce a healthy life . . . .

The way it uses the salts and waters that form its food - - - - how it detects the direction and intensity of the sun - - - and adjusts to it - - - - how it weathers the storms - - - and produces the flowers which will assure its eternity - - - - - each plant unto itself must grow . . . .

Whether it is a tiny lobelia beside a running brook - - - or a mullein that rises to great heights in the open field - - - - - - it must resist the winds - and yet - - yield to them - - - -

and it must stand again - - -

after the winds have passed . . . . .

There's splendor as each flower unfolds
    its mystic beauty to the earth . . . .
        - - - - - bright buttercups
                and daisies . . . .

- - - fringed orchises
        lovers of the swamplands - - - -
    whose tiny ballet blossoms dance with
    every breeze . . . .

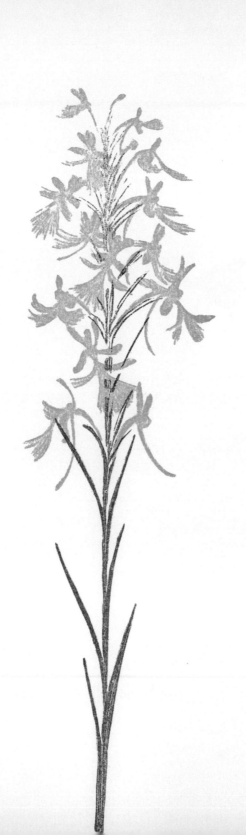

- - - - - - - - gentians' - - -

misty delicate loveliness . . . . .

- - - - - - and teasel in its armor of spines
holds heads of intricate purple flowers high in
the summer fields . . . .

and after the flowers - - -

the fruit will form . . . . . .

- - - - - - - and the seeds

and another miracle . . . . . .

Close to the land - - - and over the waters
        the air is moving - - -
                        invisibly moving - -
Far above where clouds - - and storms - - -
        and rainbows form - - - -
        the air is moving - - -
                        ever moving . . . . . .

Ripples of sunlight sparkle - -
        waves wash high on the beach
    Sandpipers teeter along the pebbles - - -
- and gulls glide with the air that is moving - -
                - - - - - always moving . . .

Softly the pine needles murmur - - - - -
        and through the branches a new moon shines
        - - - and stars . . . . . an owl soars silently
        and all around the air is moving - - -
                        gently moving . . . . .

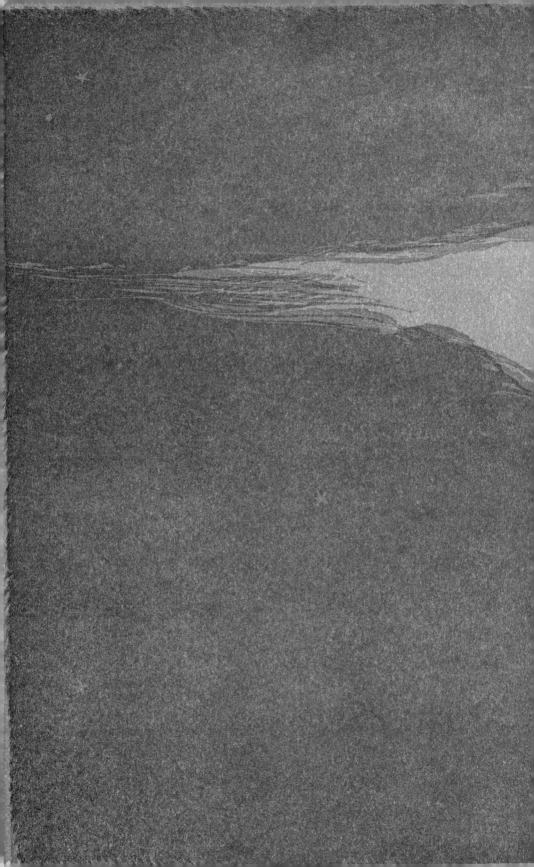

Through the azure sky little goldfinches flit
            over great waves of grass - - -
      the milkweeds are setting their seed wings free
and whimsical waves skip across still waters - - -
      as the air is moving - - - -
                        capriciously moving - - - -

Great trees sway - - - and dry leaves whirl - - -
      the swallows have flown - - -
            and wild geese fly through the air
            that is moving - - - - -
                        swiftly moving . . . . . .

Over the water the full moon rises
            into the clouds of night - - -
      faint mists of dusty greens and rusts
and dark clouds with glistening edges - - - -
      clouds that form as the air is moving - - - -
                  quietly moving . . . . . .

Forever and ever the air will be moving
            bringing the rains and the calms - - - -
      ever changing - - - and ever the same
      through the days and nights
      - - - - the heats and the colds of the years
            the air will be moving - - - - - -
                  eternally moving . . . . .

- - the ferns were the first
        great trees of earth - -
to glorious heights they grew

now - - -

    in quiet peaceful glens
    they've earned their right to solitude . . . .

Under the leaves of spring

on the damp and sheltered earth

a little brown nut cracks open . . . . . .

Into the soft earth a fine thread fastens itself - - - -
while a stem with leaves tucked inside a little shell
rises toward the sun . . . . .

Swiftly the single root reaches to greater depths as
two rust leaves open from the center of the first
seed-leaves - - - two leaves
quite different from the
nourishing embryo ones - - -
tiny miniatures of all of the
leaves this tree will grow
and drop in all its years to
come - - - - - - -

- - - - and the wondrous growth of

a great tree has begun . . . .

Each year at the end of all the twigs - a new bud will form - - - that the limbs may grow a little longer - - - - - and the tips of the branches may be forever young - - - and in the earth the roots will spread far out for the salts and water that will add another ring of growth to the trunk and every branch - twig and root . . . .

Bright warblers will come and sing their songs - - - - - and turn to inconspicuous bits of feathers - - and slip away again . . . . .

Higher and higher the young tree will reach - - - - stretching its horizontal limbs far out among the branchless trunks of older trees . . .

It will take air and water and the energy of the sun and build these things into life - - - - - the essence of its being will be growth - - - - - - self-motivated and self-sustaining - - - with no limit to the number of twigs or leaves it may produce - - - its trunk is so constructed that growth may go on indefinitely - - - - - a limb may drop in a storm - - - and it can grow another - - - as it lives in freedom to grow - - - - ever to grow . . . . - - - and because it grows luxuriously - - other life with the same staunch purpose will flourish around it . . . . .

Silently and unseen it will draw water from the earth
and return it to the air - - - - where clouds will form
and rains will refresh the land . . . . .

The winds and storms will trim its branches and shape its character - - - - - earthworms will plow and fertilize the land - - boring holes for drainage and keeping fine granular soil about its root tips - - - -

Birds will hang their nests on its branches - - - - and in turn will feed on the insects that live in its foliage Beechdrops will find nourishment on its roots - - - and Indian pipes will rise from the damp leaves at its base . .

All through its life there will be drama - - - - - the drama of life and its beauty . . . .

It will witness little comedies - - - as young things grow to make their place on earth - - - watching them frolic in the misty rain - - - - - - - - knowing them all so intimately . . . . .

It will witness the great changing of the seasons - - - - - and the loveliness of each . . .

It will witness real tragedies - - - as an insect loses its battle for life to a toad - - - - or a little bird's nest is robbed . . . . and it will live long enough to bear witness that these things are what makes life go on forever . . . .

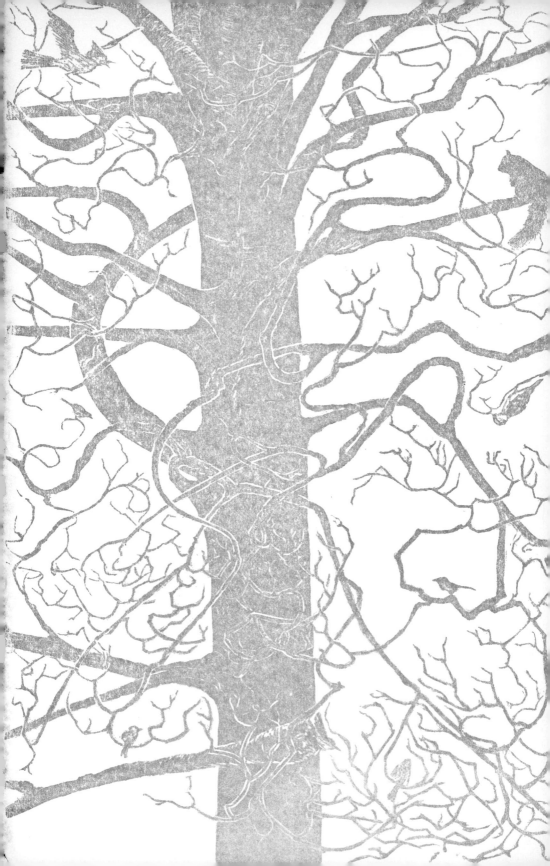

Each year it will rest - - - -

and each year its sap will rise again - - - -

its crown will be a misty gleaming web of twigs

as it stands majestic in its naked beauty . . . .

Its buds will swell - - - - -

and it will grow anew . . . .

The seasons and the years will pass - - - - -

until at last - - -

it too - - - shall fall . . . .

Mushrooms and moss will cover its trunk - - -

and it will return to earth - - -

where

. . . . another nut will open

and another tree will grow . . .

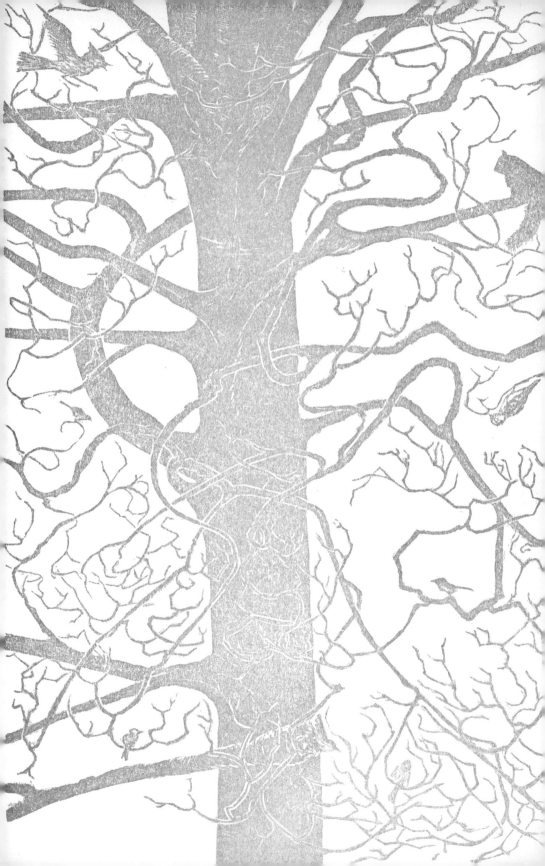